Mexicana

Albert Russo
Eric Tessier
Fray Benito Jerónimo Feijóo

Photography by Albert Russo

To order additional copies of this book, contact:
Xlibris
1-888-795-4274
www.Xlibris.com
Orders@Xlibris.com

Book Designer: Amuerfina Butron

ISBN: Softcover   978-1-4134-9062-6
         Hardcover   978-1-4134-9063-3

Library of Congress Control Number: 2005904167

Print information available on the last page

Rev. date: 10/26/2019

what's in that child's mind
whilst pigeons bask in the sun
and the world goes round?

Où court donc l'enfant
sous le regard vitreux
des deux volatiles?

¿qué buscas niña?
preguntan las palomas
tengo hambre

midday symphony
the air is still and oppressive
bliss spelled in Green

feuilles immobiles
dans la touffeur de midi
sentez donc la sève

hacen la siesta
mientras un abejorro
elige su flor

curiosity calls
for improvisation
peacefully watching

une pause au soleil
et l'on se couvre la tête
pour mieux observer

con tranquilidad
la cabeza cubierta
siguen mirando

5

the lady sells dolls
which she fashions lovingly
at the break of dawn

ces poupées
ne lui ressemblent-elles pas
elle qui les façonne?

toda su alma
en esas muñecas
ya no más huérfanas

the band has just left
her heart beats to the echoes
of its music

en quittant les lieux
ils ont semé des notes
dans son coeur

se fue la banda
sembrando en su pecho
nostalgia

7

once upon a time
the forest overwhelmed us
today we're the threat

elles prennent leurs désirs
pour des réalités
et en imposent

ni eso quedarà
de la selva ancestral
si no la cuidamos

can a menu
be more inviting?
don't pass this one!

le ventre a ses raisons
que le cuisinier connaît
montez donc ces marches!

sabiduría
de un cocinero
oaxaqueño

I really wonder
who is pulling the strings
only the puppet knows

êtes-vous sûr de savoir
qui tire les ficelles?
secret de marionnette

quién es el amo
el titiritero
o la muñeca?

artwork fashioned out
of earth's core
mischievous gaze

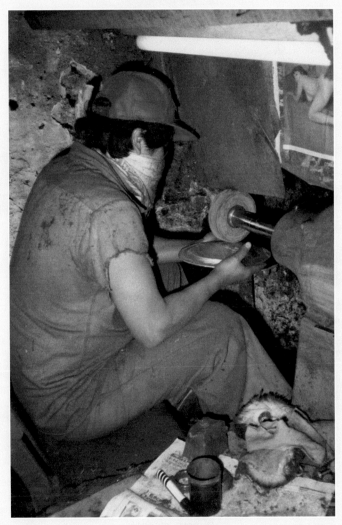

des entrailles de la terre
sortira une oeuvre d'art
elle le couve des yeux

de las entrañas
de la tierra nacerá
la obra de arte

don't listen to him
without me he's just helpless
oh yes, you can grin!

ne l'écoutez pas
sans moi il perdrait la boule
tu peux ricaner!

no lo escuchéis
lo que sabe es charlar
la dueña soy yo

young musicians
taking their cue from the elders
it is now their turn

les enfants attendent
le signal de leur aînés
pour faire leur numéro

jóvenes músicos
aguardando la señal
de sus mayores

balloons too have eyes
the vendor's engulfed in them
smothered with kisses

chorégraphie de
ballons aux yeux émerveillés
tous prêts pour l'envol

aerostáticos
envolviendo el hombre
de besos-mariposa

arms folded
they chat with the dancers
as with family

les bras croisés
ils échangent quelques mots
avec les danseurs

los brazos crusados
platican con los bailarines
de esto y de aquello

15

they're entering the scene
hearts are beating faster
silence in the square

le moment approche
les coeurs battent sourdement
lèvres scellées

dentro de poco
comienza el espectáculo
latir de corazones

quetzal feathers
adorn your heads, o proud heirs
of ancient Mexico!

vos têtes couronnées
de plumes de quetzal, ô fiers
héritiers du Mexique!

orgullosos heredores
de los dioses mexicanos
honrado el quetzal

17

sons of the jaguar
you perpetuate the rites
of the rain god

fils du jaguar
qui perpétuez les rites
du dieu de la pluie

hijos del jaguar
perpetuáis los ritos
del dios de la lluvia

they hone their craft
with clay, bird feathers and gold
competing for excellence

artisans à leur ouvrage
travaillant la glaise et l'or
des coiffes en plumes

artesanos
obrando en previsión
de la fiesta

the many facets
of industrialization
sex, the redeemer

le corps industriel
dans tous ses états
et le sexe, toujours lui

magna industria
lágrimas y sudor
el sexo sin pudor

Spanish conquerors
inflicting their brutal ways
on the 'heathen'

conquérants espagnols
imposant leur foi aux Indiens
larmes et tortures

conquistadores
arrancando el alma
de los Indios

horesemen on the way
to the Revolution
viva Zapata!

la Révolution
en marche, pour un Mexique
de sang et de liberté

jinetes en marcha
para la Revolución
qué viva México!

in full regalia
set for the ultimate fight
canine loyalty

en prévision
de la bataille décisive
loyauté canine

de punta en blanco
por la lucha decisiva
fidelidad perruna

entreating us
to act compassionately
it has a price

il nous implore
d'agir avec compassion
cela a un prix

rogándonos tratar
a nuestros pares
con compasión
eso tiene precio

the air resonates
with the joyous beat
of the mariachis

l'entraînante musique
des mariachis emplit
l'atmosphère

los mariachis
nos ofrecen
una marimba
bulliciosa

25

such an armful
of glass-beaded necklaces!
how many will she sell?

une belle brassée
de colliers de perles
il faut les écouler

tantos collares
me duelen
los brazos
¿tendré suerte?

celebrating
a wedding anniversary
at the floating gardens

on fait la fête
dans les jardins flottants
de Xochimilco

día de fiesta
en una trajinera
de Xochimilco

take your pick
my flowers are beautiful
they'll bring you luck

elles sont belles mes fleurs
elles vous porteront bonheur
n'hésitez donc pas!

comprad mis flores
os traerán amor
y fortuna

cross my heart
I shall protect you till I die
the gods be my witness!

à la vie à la mort
je serai ton protecteur
les dieux sont mes témoins

te protegeré
los dioses
son mis testigos
confía en mí

the day has come
for us to link our destinies
smile of a beetle

dans cette coccinelle
nos coeurs se scelleront
à jamais

en ese coche
se enlazarán
nuestros destinos

the air is pungent
with the scents of the tropics
and the Church looks on

l'air vibre des senteurs
entêtantes des tropiques
et l'Eglise veille

flor tras las flores
perfume embriagador
silencio cristiano

*flowery dreams, can you hear
their voices, emanating from
those white and pink gowns?*

*entendez-vous
leur cantilène au milieu
des bougainvillées?*

*¿susurro de hojas
o cantos seráficos?
todo es sueño*

art cloning life
a bird coos in the moonlight
an angel giggles

l'art clonant la vie
un oiseau chante au clair de lune
des anges passent

el arte clonando
la vida
en el claro de luna
pasa un ángel

33

arcades of prayers
they beg to be forgiven
their future crimes

arcades de prières
ils implorent le pardon
pour leurs crimes à venir

arcadas de oración
píden el perdón
para sus pecados
futuros

a touch of gold
of red tiles and lofty columns
City of Silver

des étoiles plein les yeux
tout ce qui brille à Taxco
est en argent

todo respira
lujo y tranquilidad
reino de la plata

35

flamboyant homage
to the baroque splendor of
Santo Domingo

hommage flamboyant
à la splendeur baroque de
Santo Domingo

homenaje floral
al esplandor barroco
de Santo Domingo

vestiges of
an ancient civilization
that would not die

l'âme maya
sculptée dans la pierre
imputrescible

vestigios de
una antigua civilización
que no se muere

37

out in the jungle
arose a magnificent
Mayan palace

un magnifique palais
surgi de l'enfer végétal
Palenque

El Palacio
surgido del infierno
tropical

these galleries tell
the story of a priest-king
and his mask of jade

ces galeries racontent
l'épopée d'un prêtre-roi
au masque de jade

un niño-rey
jugaba a las escondidas
con su máscara

relaxing beside
the monumental Pyramid
of the Inscriptions

moment de répit
devant la Pyramide
des Inscriptions

aflojándose
ante la Pirámide
de las Inscripciones

I wondered if
she might be reading or
just keeping accounts

je me demandais
si elle n'était pas en train de lire
ou de faire ses comptes

me preguntaba
¿está leyendo un libro
o llevando sus cuentas?

*young man waiting for
his fiancée at the market
in Mexico City*

*jeune homme attendant
sa belle sur l'esplanade
du Grand Marché*

*muchacho
esperando a su novia
en el Zócalo*

Still is the sun above our heads
No school today; an endless summer afternoon
Childhood's eternity.

Radieux et brûlant, le soleil
Un après-midi d'été, immobile et languissant,
L'éternité de l'enfance.

Fray Benito Jerónimo Feijóo

El concepto
que desde
el primer
descubrimiento
de la América
se hizo de
sus habitadores,
y aun hoy
dura entre la plebe,

Such a wide world
Are you tired, little baby?
Paradise in mommy's arms.

Un monde si vaste,
Effrayant et inconnu
Heureusement, les bras de maman.

Fray Benito Jerónimo Feijóo

es que aquella gente
no tanto se gobierna
por razón cuanto por instinto,

44

The strength of the jaguar
Has hardened my puny body
Can a fur vie with an armor?

La puissance du jaguar
Habite mon corps malingre
Mais qu'est-ce qu'une fourrure face à une
armure?

Fray Benito Jerónimo Feijóo

como si alguna
Circe, peregrinando
por aquellos
vastos países,

Multicolored leaves
The man walks the street
Stars shine in young eyes.

Comme un arbre multicolore
Sur le trottoir, l'homme magique
Et dans les yeux des enfants, des étoiles.

Fray Benito Jerónimo Feijóo

hubiese transformado
todos los hombres
en bestias.

.

Hot lava! The volcano spills
Rivers of fruit
A gift from Mother Earth.

Comme une coulée de lave brûlante
Les fruits dévalent sur les pentes du volcan,
Éventrent le marché, nous rassasient.

Fray Benito Jerónimo Feijóo

Con todo, sobran testimonios
de que su capacidad
en nada es inferior a la nuestra.

47

From the winds comes the melody
And the hearts chime along.

Vaisseau cuivré ondulant
Sur la houle des grands vents
Ils soufflent les musiques de la Terre

Fray Benito Jerónimo Feijóo

El ilustrísimo señor Palafox
no se contenta con la igualdad,

"Where is my love?
I can still feel his hands on my hips"
Alone she dances

Une danse endiablée
Si belle, si fière, figée dans sa robe de mariée
Elle ouvre le bal pour l'éternité

Fray Benito Jerónimo Feijóo

pues en el
memorial que presentó
al Rey en favor
de aquellos vasallos,
intitulado **Retrato**
natural de los indios,
dice que nos exceden.

You jumped out of darkness
In a wink you'll disappear
For one second we have been friends.

Deux créatures dans la nuit
J'ai lancé le pain, tu l'as mangé; un instant
Dans la forêt, j'ai pensé disparaître avec toi.

Fray Benito Jerónimo Feijóo

Allí cuenta
de un indio
que conoció
Su Ilustrísima,
a quien llamaban
Seis Oficios
porque otros tantos
sabía con perfección.

50

How many gallons of red wine
In your truck, officer, to fight the fire
That dries my throat?

Pompier, pour éteindre le feu qui enflamme mon gosier
Quel meilleur moyen que le vin rouge
Qui emplit la citerne de ton camion?

Fray Benito Jerónimo Feijóo

De otro que aprendió el de organero,
en cinco o seis días, sólo con observar
las operaciones del maestro,

Catching sight of you behind a window
Gives me the strength I need
No wall can stop me from reaching you.

Une simple mèche de tes cheveux entr'aperçue
Derrière une vitre me donne la force nécessaire
Aucun mur ne m'empêchera de te rejoindre.

Fray Benito Jerónimo Feijóo

sin que éste
le diese
documento alguno.
De otro que
en quince días
se hizo organista.

Like a ghost on a wall
A man's face – The fleeting image of
Freedom and Justice!

Visage spectral flottant, immatériel,
Si fragile; un rêve porteur d'espoir
Liberté et Justice – si chéries et si haïes.

Fray Benito Jerónimo Feijóo

Allí refiere también
la exquisita sutileza
con que un indio
recobró el caballo
que acababa de
robarle un español.

White as our conscience will never be
With the ideal of Purity
The angels will shed their wings.

Immaculé comme jamais notre conscience le fut
Avec la pureté comme idéal
Les anges, toujours, perdent leurs ailes.

Fray Benito Jerónimo Feijóo

Aseguraba éste,
reconvenido
por la justicia,
que el caballo
era suyo
había muchos años.

54

Life tattooed on my skin
Joyful, she dances and makes my heart beat
Cruel, she kills me with a sword

Joyeuse, elle danse sur un tambour
Marquant le rythme auquel mon cœur bat
Cruelle, elle me foudroie d'un coup d'épée.

Fray Benito Jerónimo Feijóo

El indio
no tenía testigo
alguno del robo.

55

When they destroyed the temple
The sun abandoned us and since then
Our life has been a long dull day.

Quand ils ont détruit le temple
Le soleil nous a quittés
Et avec lui le sens.

Fray Benito Jerónimo Feijóo

Viéndose en este estrecho,
prontamente echó su capa
sobre los ojos del caballo,

56

I was holding you in my arms
While an invisible orchestra was playing
Then suddenly I understood the meaning of life!

Près du kiosque à musique, notre amour
Votre sourire dans l'ombre d'un arbre
Illumine ce jour d'été.

Fray Benito Jerónimo Feijóo

y volviéndose
al español
le dijo que ya que
tanto tiempo había
era dueño
del caballo

She is carrying her stall on her head
Two baskets full of wares
Nothing must remain.

Deux paniers d'osier, ça suffit pour un étal
Comme tous les matins le marché s'installe
Tout doit disparaître.

Fray Benito Jerónimo Feijóo

no podía menos
de saber
de qué ojo
era tuerto,
así, que lo dijese;

*It's still early
But they're already at work
A new day is beginning under a lazy sun.*

*Le soleil encore endormi et l'eau fraîche qui
lave le trottoir
Premiers efforts, premiers mots échangés
Une nouvelle journée commence.*

Fray Benito Jerónimo Feijóo

*el español,
sorprendido
y turbado,
a Dios y a dicha,
respondió
que del derecho.*

So intense is our love,
On the bench we sit
Invisible to the world

Un amour si intense
Enlacés sur le banc
Nous regardons passer le monde, invisibles.

Fray Benito Jerónimo Feijóo

Entonces el indio, quitando la capa,
mostró al juez y a todos los asistentes

They say dad was a rotten yobbo
And mum a vicious one. Let them talk!
Did they think I had no future?

Selon eux papa était pourri
Et maman vicieuse. Laissez-les dire.
Qui penserait que je n'ai pas d'avenir?

Fray Benito Jerónimo Feijóo

que el caballo no era tuerto
ni de uno ni de otro ojo;

Pleasure and hell in my hand
Such a tiny weapon
Red chilli.

Si petit dans ma main
Comme un insecte sans défense, et pourtant...
Un piment.

Fray Benito Jerónimo Feijóo

y convencido
el español
del robo,
se le restituyó
el caballo
al indio.

62

What a perfect moment!
you looked like a goddess in the sun.
Then, suddenly, we became human
Strictly human, you and I,
Here, in the staircase...

La beauté d'un moment parfait;
un amour, Madame,
Pur, radieux, et puis, soudain,
l'irrépressible besoin
De vous bousculer sans façon,
Là, dans l'escalier... tout de suite!

Fray Benito Jerónimo Feijóo

Apenas los españoles,
debajo de la conducta
de Cortés,
entraron en América,

Wandering in the ruins
The ghosts of the Inquisition
Tormented by the memory of their crimes

Errant dans les ruines
Les fantômes de l'Inquisition
Tourmentés par le souvenir de leurs crimes.

Fray Benito Jerónimo Feijóo

cuando tuvieron
muchas ocasiones
de conocer que
aquellos naturales
eran de la misma
especie que ellos
e hijos del
mismo Padre.

64

Children of ancient times
They come, invincible
To perpetuate the old rites

Un campement sur la pierre ou le béton
Au beau milieu de la ville
Les lieux sacrés, toujours.

Fray Benito Jerónimo Feijóo

Léense en la historia
de la conquista
de Méjico

65

The exit was in sight
But the few yards we had to walk through
Could be the most dangerous we'd ever face.

La sortie nous narguait, là-bas
Si proche, mais les quelques mètres à parcourir
Pour y parvenir pouvaient s'avérer mortels.

Fray Benito Jerónimo Feijóo

estratagemas militares
de aquella gente
nada inferiores
a las de Cartagineses,
griegos y romanos.

A symphony of colors
And scents; and there, in the middle, stands
Our Holy Lady, the queen of harvest .

Symphonie de couleurs
Et d'odeurs; trônant au milieu
Celle qui, depuis toujours, nous nourrit.

Fray Benito Jerónimo Feijóo

Muchos han observado
que los criollos,
o hijos de españoles,

67

So you don't believe in hell!
How silly!
Where do you think you're living?

Ainsi tu ne crois pas à l'enfer!
Comme c'est étrange!
Mais où donc crois-tu vivre?

Fray Benito Jerónimo Feijóo

que nacen en aquella tierra
son de mas viveza o agilidad intelectual
que los que produce España.

Poverty and chastity
Gold and silver
How they suffer!

Vœu de pauvreté
Parmi l'or et la magnificence des églises
Ils souffrent.

Fray Benito Jerónimo Feijóo

Lo que añaden otros
que aquellos ingenios
así como amanecen
más temprano

Some rooms in the basement
Were crawling with carnivorous centipedes
We had to lock them in.

Certaines pièces en sous-sol
Grouillaient de vermines carnivores
Et nous devions les condamner.

Fray Benito Jerónimo Feijóo

también
se anochecen
mas presto;
no sé que esté
justificado.

70

Listen to the stones
They're telling us about
Our past.

Ecoutez la voix des pierres
Elle nous parle
De notre passé.

Fray Benito Jerónimo Feijóo

Es discurrir groseramente
hacer bajo concepto
de la capacidad de los indios

How can we live while
Our brother is starving?
How can we justify such indifference?

Comment peut-on vivre
Pendant qu'un frère crève de faim?
Comment peut-on justifier notre indifférence?

Fray Benito Jerónimo Feijóo

porque al principio
daban pedazos de oro
por cuentas de vidrio.

72

*A face in the crowd
Beauty suddenly materializing
A moment in time.*

*Un visage dans la foule
Surgi de nulle part
Moment de bonheur.*

Fray Benito Jerónimo Feijóo

*Más rudo es que ellos
quien por esto
los juzga rudos.*

He blows in his trumpet
Then all over Mexico
Rings the voice of humanity.

Soudain il saisit sa trompette et souffle
A travers tout le Mexique, alors,
Chacun peut entendre chanter l'humanité.

Fray Benito Jerónimo Feijóo

Si se mira sin prevención,
más hermoso
es el vidrio que el oro;

Flowers all around
And the sound of your laughter
A garden that is larger than the whole world.

Ce jardin, entre ses quatre murs
Si plein de fleurs et de ta gaieté
Est plus vaste que le monde lui-même.

Fray Benito Jerónimo Feijóo

y en lo que
se busca
para ostentación
y adorno,
en igualdad
de hermosura,
siempre se prefiere
lo más raro.

Wherever a man says
NO
Stands Democracy.

Partout où un homme dit
NON
Vit la démocratie.

Fray Benito Jerónimo Feijóo

No hacían, pues, en esto los americanos
otra cosa que lo que hace todo el mundo.

What do you sell?
Potatoes or nuggets? He smiles:
"Have a cigar, my friend."

Que vendez-vous?
Des pommes de terre ou des pépites?
Il sourit: "Prenez donc un cigare, mon ami."

Fray Benito Jerónimo Feijóo

Teman oro y no vidrio;

Is it only a show?
That's what the audience thinks
But the ancient gods still hear the prayer of the devoted.

On pourrait croire que ce n'est qu'un spectacle
Et c'en est un réellement, mais pas uniquement
Les anciens dieux écoutent toujours la prière des hommes.

Fray Benito Jerónimo Feijóo

por eso era entre ellos,
y con razon,

78

Incense and procession
A choir sings
Faith is alive.

Odeur d'encens
Chants fervents
La foi est vivante.

Fray Benito Jerónimo Feijóo

más digna alhaja
de una Princesa

It's closing time.
How was your day?
As sunny as my night will be still

Nous fermons.
La journée a été bonne?
Aussi bonne que va l'être notre soirée.

Fray Benito Jerónimo Feijóo

un pequeño collar de cuentas de vidrio
que una gran cadena de oro …

AUTHORS / AUTEURS / AUTORES

Albert Russo has written many books in English, published by Domhan Books and Xlibris, namely *The Age of the Pearl, Beyond the Great Water, Oh Zaperetta!* and *The Benevolent American in the Heart of Darkness*. His fiction and poetry appear in English and in French around the world; his work has been translated into a dozen languages. His literary website: www.albertrusso.com

Albert Russo a écrit de nombreux romans, ainsi que des recueils de nouvelles et de poésie, en français et en anglais. Son oeuvre a été traduite dans une douzaine de langues. En France, ses derniers livres sont publiés aux éditions Hors Commerce, dont *L'ancêtre noire et La Tour Shalom*. Son site littéraire: www.albertrusso.com

Albert Russo. Nació en Congo/Zaïre. Escribe narrativa y poesía en inglés y en francés. Su obra está traducida en una docena de idiomas en los cinco continentes. Obras principales - en francés: *Sang Mêlé ou ton fils Léopold, L'ancêtre noire y La Tour Shalom* - en inglés: *Oh Zaperetta! , The Benevolent American in the Heart of Darkness y The Crowded World of Solitude* (cuentos y poesia). Su sitio: www.albertrusso.com

ooo

Eric Tessier has published several collections of short stories in French. He is the editor of the literary magazine La Nef Des Fous. He also contributes regularly to The Taj Mahal Review (India) and to Skyline Magazine (NY - USA)

Eric Tessier est l'auteur de 3 recueils de nouvelles parus aux éditions Editinter et Rafael de Surtis. Il dirige la revue La Nef Des Fous.

Eric Tessier. Nació en Francia. Redactor de la revista La Nef Des Fous, ha publicado cuentos en francés y en inglés en Europa, India y Estados Unidos. Ha editado tres libros de cuentos en Francia.

ooo

Fray Benito Jerónimo Feijóo (1676-1764). One of Spain's major essayists of the 18th century, he strongly denounced the conquistadors' harsh treatment of the native Indian populations of Peru and Mexico.

Fray Benito Jerónimo Feijóo (1676-1764). Sans doute l'essayiste espagnol le plus important du 18e siècle, il critiqua sévèrement la politique des conquistadors à l'encontre des Indiens du Pérou et du Mexique.

Fray Benito Jerónimo Feijóo (1676-1764). Es, quizá, el escritor ibérico más importante del siglo XVIII. El fué quien, con su crítica, abrió en España las puertas a las ideas modernas haciendo así posible que la cultura española saliese del estancamiento en que se hallaba despué de la gran Edad de Oro. Ensayos principales: *Cartas eruditas, Mapa intelectual y cotejo de naciones*, etcétera.

ooo

Other artbooks, completing the series, published with Xlibris, by the same authors, in English, French and Italian:
ROMAdiva, Chinese puzzle, AfricaSoul, In France.

Printed in the United States
By Bookmasters